D1093155

STAFFORDSHIRE BULL TERRIER

INTERPET
PUBLISHING

Introduction

Bulldogs, Mastiffs, British working terriers, Pointers and Dalmatians are among the ancestors of today's Staffordshire Bull Terriers. The Staffy inherited courage and intelligence from this varied ancestry, but the breed has a fervent love of people and children that is all its own. Staffies gradually became popular with a wide cross section of British society and have now become the fifth most popular dog in the country. British and Irish workers took Staffies over to America in the late nineteenth century. The breed won its first official recognition at the Crufts' show of 1936. Most Staffies enjoy good and robust health and live for between ten and sixteen years but need plenty of regular exercise to keep them calm and happy.

Published by Interpet Publishing,
Vincent Lane, Dorking,
Surrey, RH4 3YX, UK.

© 2014 Interpet Publishing. All rights reserved

ISBN 978 1 84286 2506

Printed and bound in China

Contents

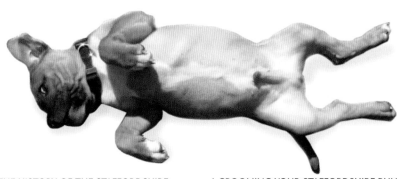

ABOVE: *Mastiffs were originally bred to hunt stags and wild boars and the Staffy has retained some of their traits.*

1 THE HISTORY OF THE STAFFORDSHIRE BULL TERRIER

Today's Staffordshire Bull Terriers are the result of cross between several different types of dog. These ancestral dogs included Bulldogs, Mastiffs and various British working terriers, including the Manchester Terrier and the (now extinct) English White Terrier. Mastiffs were originally bred to hunt stags and wild boars and the Staffy has retained some of their traits. Pointer and Dalmatian DNA may also have been introduced into the breed. Ultimately, two basic dog types resulted from this intermingling of several breeds, the Bull and Terrier and the Pit Bull. Ultimately, only the Bull and Terrier was recognized by the British Kennel Club.

Bull and Terriers and Pit Bulls were originally bred and used for bull and bear-baiting. These early dogs were larger and more heavily muscled than today's Staffies. The cruel and horribly violent practice of baiting involved packs of dogs being set on bulls and bears. Naturally, these dogs needed massive courage to attack these large and heavy animals that were more than twenty times their size in weight. Baiting supposedly

tenderised the animals' meat through adrenaline and nor-adrenaline being released into the flesh. But in reality baiting became an excuse for a grim and bloody "sporting" spectacle. This horrible practice is still carried on in some parts of the world.

As bull baiting declined in popularity during the seventeenth century, dog fighting became more popular. Unfortunately, Staffordshire Bull Terriers were considered ideal for this "sport," with their athletic bodies, powerful heads, strength, courage and agility. Their in-built aggression towards other animals (from their baiting days) made them ideal for fighting.

ABOVE: *Good with children, Staffordshire Bull Terriers became known as the Nanny Dog.*

ABOVE: *The breed soon gained popularity with aristocrats and working men alike.*

The dogs of this era were smaller and stockier than the dogs that had been used for baiting and were much more agile. The quality of "gameness" became highly prized in these fighting dogs. Although Staffordshire Bull Terriers were ferocious fighting dogs they also made loyal pets and were wonderful with children. In fact, dogs of the breed are so good with children that Staffordshire Bull Terriers became known as the Nanny Dog.

As time went on, Staffordshire Bull Terriers became popular with a wide cross section of British society. Several aristocrats including Lord Camelford owned examples of the breed.

Camelford had a famous Staffordshire Bull Terrier known as Belcher. The breed was also a favourite with the working classes including miners, chain-makers, Staffordshire potters and steelworkers from Britain's industrial Black Country. Some of these less well off owners used their dogs to make a little money from dog fighting, badger baiting or vermin control. Ironically, although these animals were bred to be aggressive towards other dogs, dogs that showed vicious tendencies to human beings were destroyed. Over time this meant that the breed became increasingly friendly and loving to people, a characteristic that is

ABOVE: *it is extremely important to socialise Staffies with other dogs at an early age.*

very evident today. The breed's other temperamental characteristics have also been retained by the Staffords of today. For this reason, it is extremely important to socialise Staffies with other dogs at an early age to ensure that they can be trusted around other dogs when they grow up.

By the middle of the nineteenth century, dog fighting went underground after it was outlawed by the Humane Act of 1835. But the dog owners of Staffordshire preserved the breed with careful breeding that was designed to retain its special character. Over time, this selective breeding meant that the Staffordshire Bull Terrier became a defined and recognizable breed. The first breed club was formed in Staffordshire in 1935 and the dogs finally acquired their formal nomenclature of the

Staffordshire Bull Terrier. The first breed standard was drawn up in 1935 at the Old Cross Guns public house in the West Midlands. It was written by a group of around thirty Staffordshire Bull Terrier enthusiasts. The club's first secretary was a local Staffordshire man, Joseph Dunn.

Staffordshire Bull Terriers were first shown at the famous Crufts dog show in 1936. The breed's first official recognition came in 1938 at a Championship show held in Birmingham, England. It was here that the first two breed champions were chosen. These were the bitch Lady Eve and the dog Gentleman Jim. Both dogs had been bred by the Staffordshire breed club secretary Joseph Dunn.

Several Staffordshire Bull Terriers also made their way over to the United States in the late nineteenth century with British and Irish workers that emigrated across the Atlantic and took their dogs with them. These dogs are the ancestors of several American breeds including the Yankee Terrier, the American Bull Terrier and the American Pit Bull Terrier.

Although the Staffordshire Terrier Club of America was founded on May 23 1936 to protect the "Grand Old Breed," Staffords were not formally recognized by the American Kennel Club until 1975. At the same time, the AKC also recognized the American Staffordshire Terrier. This breed is shorter-legged and thicker set than the Staffordshire Bull Terrier. The first registered American Staffordshire Bull Terrier was Champion Tinkinswood Imperial, a dog that had been imported from Britain. The first American champion Staffordshire Bull Terrier was Northwark Becky Sharpe, a dog that had been imported from Australia.

In the UK, the breed went from strength to strength in the

ABOVE: *Staffordshire Bull Terriers were first shown at the famous Crufts dog show in 1936.*

RIGHT: *Dog fighting was outlawed by the Humane Act of 1835.*

11

twentieth century and became increasingly popular. In the 1980s British Staffordshire Bull Terriers were interbred with Staffordshire Bull Terriers from Ireland and this strain became known as the Irish Staffordshire Bull Terriers.

The Staffordshire Bull Terrier is now one of the most popular terriers in Britain, with fifteen active breed clubs. They are also one of the ten most popular dogs in Australia, and are the most popular terrier in South Africa. Although Staffords are now well established in America, the American Pit Bull Terrier is more popular there.

Staffies are now highly regarded by many people and have a wonderful reputation for their indomitable

courage, intelligence, and affectionate nature with children. The British Kennel Club describes the breed as "Bold, fearless and totally reliable." It is one of only two breeds that are officially recognized by the Kennel Club as being good with children. Despite this, the fact that Staffordshire Bull Terriers bear a superficial resemblance to some of the dogs covered by the 1991 Dangerous Dogs Act has caused a great deal of reputational damage to the breed. The dogs actually covered by this Act are the Pit Bull Terrier, the Japanese Tosa, the Dogo Argentino and the Fila Brasileiro. The confusion is intensified by the fact that Pit Bull Terriers and Dogo Argentinos are sometimes passed off as Staffordshire

ABOVE: *Staffords were not formally recognized by the American Kennel Club until 1975.*

Bull Terriers by their owners, to prevent them from being destroyed (one of the sanctions of the Act). The Act makes the ownership of these four breeds punishable by a fine or imprisonment. Under the terms of the Act, the British Government also discourages the importation of the American Staffordshire Terrier and, as the names of the breeds are so similar, this has also conspired to damage the Staffie's reputation.

Despite this completely undeserved negative publicity, Staffordshire Bull Terriers are now the fifth most popular dog in the United Kingdom. Although Staffordshire Bull Terriers make up a sadly disproportionate number of the

dogs in re-homing centres, they also have a great reputation as fantastic family pets that adore their families and are wonderful around children. Ironically, this love of people means that Staffordshire Bull Terriers don't usually make good guard dogs.

Most Staffies enjoy good health and usually live for between ten and sixteen years. They don't usually have any special dietary requirements and are generally quite hardy. Staffies do need plenty of exercise, but with their muscular bodies and high intelligence, they can excel at Agility, Flyball and Obedience competitions.

2 CHOOSING YOUR STAFFORDSHIRE BULL TERRIER

Staffordshire Bull Terriers have suffered from irresponsible breeding in recent years, and you should take care that the puppy you are considering giving a home to is not the result of puppy farming. It is very important that you source your dog from a reputable breeder. Bringing any dog into your life is a serious undertaking, but Staffords have had so much undeserved bad press that it is particularly important when considering a dog of this breed. Responsible breeders of Staffordshire Bull Terriers don't advertise in classified newspapers, dog magazines, or posters in local shops, as they want to discourage impulse buying. They want to find good, permanent homes for their puppies with owners that have a good idea of the commitment that a Staffordshire Bull Terrier requires. Shelters and rescue centres are full of Staffies that were bought on the spur of the moment and no responsible breeder wants to see their animals abandoned in this way. The fact that the breed has received quite a lot of negative feedback in the press means that responsible Staffy ownership is even more crucial than ever. A good owner will be able to repair some of the undeserved damage to the reputation of the breed.

Staffies really need their daily exercise even more than many other dog breeds. They have high energy levels and the more exercise they get the calmer and better behaved they will be. In an ideal world, a fully-grown Staffordshire Bull Terrier needs around forty-five minutes of exercise two to three times a day. You should always keep your dog on his leash in public. Staffies can become nervous and excitable when they are around people they don't know. Although this is a

big commitment, you will find that the saying "a tired dog is a good dog" is particularly true of this breed. Of course, you will need to tailor the level of exercise that you give your dog to take into account his age, fitness and individual temperament. Dogs that do not get enough exercise will almost inevitably become restless and hard to train. At worst, they may even become aggressive.

Staffordshire Bull Terriers are also intelligent dogs that require mental stimulation. Obedience training, learning tricks or playing with interesting toys will help him to feel calm and satisfied with life.

As with any puppy, it is important to build your bond with your Staffy. Activities that you can do together, like jogging or playing flying disk will help you to build this connection with your new dog. Although Staffies love play and attention, he will also need some time to himself. A (genuinely) robust toy that it is safe for him to play with by himself may help him to enjoy this alone time more.

For their own safety, Staffies need to have a well-secured environment. These dogs can both dig under and jump over low barriers, and have the reputation of being excellent escape artists.

ABOVE: *Responsible breeders of Staffordshire Bull Terriers want to find good, permanent homes for their puppies.*

Plenty of human companionship will be crucial to the happiness of your Staffy, and he certainly would not enjoy being left along for long periods of time. No dog should be treated like this, as loneliness will almost certainly lead to bad behaviour. Strong dogs like these can inflict a lot of damage if they become bored and destructive. If you need to leave your dog to go to work you should arrange for some human companionship and exercise for him during the day. It is worth remembering, however, that it is human companionship that Staffies really crave. They don't particularly need the company of other dogs.

They will usually tolerate other dogs in their home environment, although their extremely strong bond with their human family can sometimes lead to jealous quarrels between co-habiting Staffies.

A very important consideration when deciding to buy a Staffordshire Bull Terrier is that these dogs need to be really well socialised with other dogs at as early an age as possible. You will need to make a really good effort to take your dog to puppy classes as regularly as possible and to as many public places as you can. This should curb any problems of aggression towards other dogs in the future.

ABOVE: *Staffordshire Bull Terriers need to be really well socialised with other dogs at an early age.*

16

Dog or Bitch?

The personality differences between male and female Staffordshire Bull Terriers are quite significant. Dogs tend to be more dominant and will need more positive leadership from you. Dogs can be quite dominant towards other dogs and will often want to be the leader of the pack. Bitches tend to be more submissive and will look to their owners to be their pack leader. If you want to have two Staffordshire Bull Terriers, a dog and a bitch will probably get on best. Two dominant males may fight, and two dominant bitches may also be aggressive to one another. Because of these tendencies, some experienced owners prefer to sleep their Staffies in different rooms at night. Buying Staffords one at a time, and adding a new dog to the family only when a firm bond with the original dog has been established is usually considered to be more successful than buying two littermates.

PET OR SHOW DOG?
Although Staffordshire Bull Terriers have become increasingly popular at dog shows, most Staffords are initially bought as family and/or companion animals. To become a show dog, your puppy and his parents must all be registered with the Kennel Club. He must also be one of the six approved colours for showing; solid red, fawn, white, black, blue or brindle. Puppies need to be at least six months old before they can enter the show ring, and must have had their first vaccinations. Large shows can be quite daunting for young dogs and it might be useful to get some basic experience at your local breed club before going into the ring.

17

Puppy or Older Dog?

ABOVE: *Breeding bitches may need a home when they are retired.*

One of the great things about adopting a grown-up Staffordshire Bull Terrier is that you are probably giving a home to a dog that really needs one. This is particularly true for this breed, where so many dogs of all ages are abandoned. There are many Staffy rescue organisations with dogs available in Britain, the United States and Canada. There will also be advantages to you. Your older dog may well be house trained (or nearly house trained!) and may also have been taught how to walk on the lead, and ride in the car. You can also see exactly what you are getting in the way of temperament and size. The best way to find an older Stafford may be through a breed rescue organisation. Dogs can end up in rescue kennels for many reasons, most of which are not any fault of the dog. For example, the dog's owner may have died or become ill, or a dog bought for showing may not have reached the required standard. Divorce and family breakdown can also result in dogs being left homeless. Breeding bitches and stud dogs may also need to find a "forever" home of their own once they have been retired from producing puppies.

As a breed, Staffordshire Bull Terriers have also suffered from over-breeding and irresponsible ownership. This problem has been highlighted by the British RSPCA, which has established "Team Staffy" to promote the positive aspects of the breed. The organisation has also made a great video called "Britain, Love Your Staffy!" There are several organisations in America and Britain that specialize in re-homing abandoned Staffies and finding these great dogs the loving and responsible families that they deserve.

RIGHT: *Re-homing an older dog can be done through rescue organisations for this breed.*

Puppy Staffordshire Bull Terrier

If you decide to buy a puppy Staffordshire Bull Terrier, you will need to find a highly regarded and responsible breeder. One of the best ways to do this is to contact a Stafford breed club. Breed clubs often have lists of litters that have been bred by their members. If you can, it is highly

BELOW: *It is always good to see the home conditions of a litter before you choose your puppy.*

ABOVE: *Children should be supervised when playing with your Staffy.*

desirable to meet the breeder before you decide to buy. A good breeder will want to know that you can offer a good home to one of their puppies and this will give you a chance to see the conditions in which your pup has been bred. Another good way of contacting breeders is to visit dog shows where Staffordshire Bull Terriers are being shown. This would also give you a wonderful opportunity of meeting some Staffies close up and seeing the different sexes, sizes, and colours of the breed. The UK Kennel Club also has the Assured Breeder scheme where their members can offer litters on-line through their website. This is an excellent way of buying a dog for

showing if that is your ambition.

But the very best way to find your puppy is by personal recommendation from someone who has already bought a puppy from a breeder. If you are looking for a Staffy to be a loving pet and companion, you need to look for a puppy from an affectionate and healthy environment.

A good breeder will also want to make sure that they are placing their puppies in good homes and should ask many questions about your home environment and lifestyle. If they do not feel that you can offer one of their puppies a good home, they may even refuse to sell you one. A responsible breeder will be particularly concerned

ABOVE: *Word of mouth is a good way to find a reputable breeder.*

to find out that you will be able to give your Staffy all the exercise he needs, and that you are aware that your dog will need to be socialised with other dogs from an early age. Many Staffords that end up in rescue centres have been sold into homes that were completely unsuitable for them for one reason or another, and a good breeder will try to avoid this as much as possible.

If you are lucky enough to find a litter that has the kind of pup you are looking for, it can be a great bonding experience to meet your future puppy a couple of times before you take him home with you. It will also give you a chance to meet the parents of your puppy (or the dam at least) and this will give you an idea of how your dog will develop. You can also keep an eye on him to make sure that he stays in good health before you pick him up. This should be at around eight weeks old. A good breeder will be happy to welcome you to see your puppy and will be pleased by your interest in their dogs.

ABOVE: *Meeting the parents will give you an idea of the puppy's temperament.*

Choosing Your Puppy

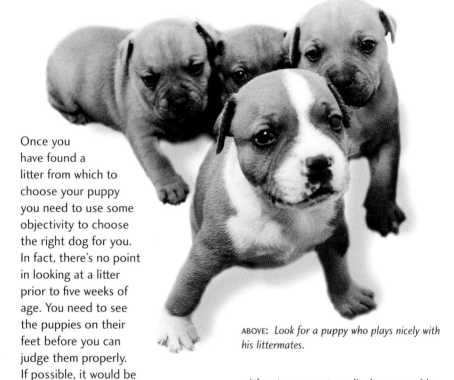

Once you have found a litter from which to choose your puppy you need to use some objectivity to choose the right dog for you. In fact, there's no point in looking at a litter prior to five weeks of age. You need to see the puppies on their feet before you can judge them properly. If possible, it would be great to see the puppies' mother and father. The main points to look for are your puppy's physical and behavioural health.

ABOVE: *Look for a puppy who plays nicely with his littermates.*

So far as his physical health goes, there are several things that you should look out for. The puppy should have a good level of energy, and appear alert and interested in his surroundings. His eyes should be bright and clear without any crust or discharge, and he should be able to see a ball that rolls by slowly. His nose should not be dry or crusty and his ears should look and smell clean. The puppy should be able to hear you if you clap behind his head. He should look well fed, and have a little fat over his ribs. A healthy puppy's bottom should be free from faeces. His coat should be flat and glossy and

ABOVE: *Wait until a puppy is at least five weeks old before you make your selection.*

not scurfy, dull or greasy. There should be no evidence of fleas or lice in his coat. He should be able to walk freely without any limping or discomfort, but don't be worried if the puppies appear "knobbly kneed" as this is quite normal. You should also check the puppy for hernias; he should not have any odd lumps or bumps in his tummy. If you are buying a dog, you can see if his testicles have dropped into place. This sometimes doesn't happen until the dog is a little older, so don't panic if you can't feel them.

If you have a particular Staffy colour in mind, you may need to go looking for a breeder that specialises in dogs of this colour. Some litters are blends of mixed red and brindle puppies, or coloured and pied dogs.

So far as behaviour goes, you should look for a puppy that seems to be interacting well with his littermates

– playing nicely without being too assertive. The puppy should also be interested in playing with you and should approach you willingly. He should be happy about being handled, and let you cuddle him and touch him all over his body. If he remains calm and relaxed while do this, he is likely to be easier to handle when he grows up. A passive but outgoing and happy puppy who can live comfortably with other species will be an easy dog to live with. A very boisterous or timid puppy will probably be the same when he grows up. If you can, it is very helpful to spend a little time with the puppy's parents and gauge how they react to you and your family. If you don't like their temperament, you shouldn't buy one of their puppies. Your final decision should be based on finding a puppy that reacts well to you and your family, especially if you have children.

3 CARING FOR YOUR STAFFORDSHIRE BULL TERRIER PUPPY

PUPPY EQUIPMENT

Before you collect your puppy, you will need to equip yourself with some simple pup-friendly equipment. His requirements will include a bed, basket, or dog crate, a puppy collar and lead, a grooming brush, safe, durable puppy-friendly toys and puppy food (as per the breeder's instructions). Stainless steel dishes are ideal for your puppy's food and won't be chewed to destruction.

PREPARING FOR YOUR PUPPY

You will need to make some important preparations before you collect your puppy and bring him home. You need to decide where you want your puppy to sleep, eat and exercise and which parts of your house you will allow the puppy to go. Consistent behaviour on your part will help your puppy feel secure and settle down quickly, so start as you mean to go on. All dogs need to have a routine and it is best to get this

ABOVE: *Introduce your puppy to the other members of the family.*

DANGEROUS PLANTS FOR DOGS

Many house and garden plants are also highly toxic to dogs and puppies, and you should be very careful to keep them away from your Stafford at any age. Of course puppies are much more likely to chew unsuitable things, so you need to be particularly careful that they are not exposed to a whole list of dangerous plant materials including:

ACONITES	AVOCADO	CLEMATIS	MISTLETOE
AFRICAN VIOLETS	BLUEBELLS	COCOA HUSKS (used in garden mulches)	ONIONS
APPLE SEEDS	BOX WOOD		RAGWORT
APRICOT STONES	BUTTERCUPS	DAFFODIL BULBS	RHUBARB
CROCUSES	CHERRY STONES	ELEPHANT EARS	WILD CHERRY
	CHRISTMAS ROSES	IVY	YEW

established as soon as possible.

Before you collect your puppy you must make sure that his new environment is free of any hidden hazards. Very importantly, your garden needs to be well fenced. A little Staffy puppy is very strong and needs only a tiny hole to squeeze through. Any openwork gates should have wire mesh attached, and any dangerous garden equipment should be put away. Ponds are a particular hazard for puppies. If they fall in, they may well be unable to climb out. Indoors, you must make sure that electrical cables and television and phone wires are concealed and

any rubbish is kept out of his way. You should also remove anything that could become a choking hazard, such as string, rubber bands or small toys. Dangerous foods should also be kept well away from your dog. These include chocolate, onions, garlic, apple and pear pips, plum peach and apricot stones, potato peelings, alcohol, tea, coffee, raisins and grapes. All of these are poisonous to dogs. It goes without saying that rodent poison can be fatal to dogs and shouldn't be used anywhere in the dog's environment.

Home security is also an important issue, as many puppies are stolen from

BELOW: *When preparing for your puppy's arrival, remember that puppies are great escape artists.*

their homes every year. It is a good idea to check the garden perimeter every day and make sure that the gates are shut and bolted. Automatic closers on your doors and gates are a great idea to prevent them being left open by visitors.

It is also a good idea to put away anything you don't want to be chewed. Staffies have a knack of chewing exactly the wrong thing and you don't want to be telling off your new puppy on his first day in his new home. It might be a good idea to confine your Staffy puppy to a metal or plastic puppy pen to keep him as safe as possible.

One of the most important things to decide is where your puppy is going to sleep. This is crucial as this is somewhere that your puppy needs to feel completely safe and secure. It should be a place that suits both you and the dog. The most important thing is that the sleeping area should be warm, dry and completely draught free. Many owners prefer their new puppies to sleep in the kitchen or utility room as these rooms usually have washable floors. But you should not let him sleep in a confined space where there is a boiler in case of carbon monoxide leaks. For the same reason, you should not leave your dog in the kitchen if you leave something cooking in the oven while you are out. You could also fence off a small area around the basket with his puppy pen so that your puppy won't be able to get into trouble in

ABOVE: *The dog crate should always be a safe refuge for your dog and never used as punishment.*

the night. A dog crate or cage can also make your dog feel comfortable and secure. If you leave the door open, your dog can also use the crate as his refuge during the day. Dog crates are also useful to keep your dog confined and safe during car journeys. You should never use the crate to punish your dog, as he should always want to go into it.

Although there are many different kinds of dog beds on the market, the simple plastic kidney-shaped baskets, which come in many different sizes and colours, are some of the most practical.

ABOVE: *A plastic dog bed is easy to keep clean and can be made snug with a fleece pad.*

They resist chewing and can be washed and disinfected. They can also be filled with cozy pads or mattresses on which the puppy can sleep comfortably. These mattress inserts can usually be washed in the washing machine. It's a good idea to buy two of these in case of accidents! An excellent idea is to replace the fabric softener in the washing cycle with a slug of disinfectant to make sure that any germs or bad smells are destroyed. Wicker baskets can be dangerous when chewed as the sharp sticks can damage the puppy's mouth or throat. Equally, bean bag beds can easily be chewed through and the polystyrene beans they contain are difficult to clean up. Dog duvets are equally prone to chewing.

COLLECTING YOUR PUPPY

The best age to collect your puppy is when he is around eight weeks old. When you arrange a time to pick him up from the breeder, a time around mid-morning is often the most convenient. This will give the puppy a good chance to feel at home by bedtime. He will be able to sniff around his new home, be cuddled by his new owners, eat, play and sleep before he faces the night alone.

It's a good idea to take someone with you when you go to collect your Staffy puppy, so that one of you can drive and the other one can comfort the pup. An old towel to mop up any accidents is a good idea. When you collect him, make sure that you find out when he will need his next worming treatment and what vaccinations he has had. You should also receive a copy of your puppy's pedigree.

Although it is a very exciting time when you bring your Stafford home for the first time, you should try to keep the atmosphere as calm and reassuring as possible. Moving to his new home is a complete change for your puppy and he has to fit into a completely new environment. If there are other animals in your home you should always supervise the puppy until they have settled down together. Alternatively, if you are re-homing an older dog, he may already have insecurities that you will need to dispel. A kind, firm and calm approach works best.

ABOVE: *Your puppy will want to explore his new home.*

ABOVE: *After the excitement of his first day at home your puppy will be tired by bedtime.*

ABOVE: *Staffies really love their owners!*

LIFE CHANGES

Your puppy will have a lot of things to adjust to. At first, he may well feel lonely without his littermates around him. A hot water bottle wrapped up in a blanket and a cuddly toy may help. Beware of going to your puppy if he cries during his first night with you. This is giving him the message that you will come running whenever he cries. You may also be tempted to take a miserable puppy into your own bed which you may not want to do in the long-term. A half-way house is to allow the puppy to sleep in a high-sided box in your room so that you can comfort any crying. The box will mean that he has to stay put and can't get into

difficulties or fall down the stairs. After a couple of days, you can move your Staffy puppy into the kitchen.

If you are re-homing an older dog, be sure to call him by the name he is used to. Trying to change it to something you prefer will confuse and upset him.

INOCULATIONS

One of the first and most important things you need to do for your puppy Stafford is to make sure that he is enrolled into a comprehensive vaccination programme. This will protect him against the serious illnesses of canine distemper, infectious hepatitis, parvovirus, leptospirosis and kennel cough. He will need regular boosters throughout his life, at least once a year. You should keep your puppy at home until he is fully protected. Because your puppy's socialisation should ideally begin before he will have been fully vaccinated, it may be a good idea to invite friends who have fully vaccinated and healthy dogs to meet him at your home.

Puppies should be vaccinated at 6–9 weeks of age and then again at 10–12 weeks. Puppies usually become fully protected two weeks after the second vaccination but your vet may recommend a third dose for some puppies. The vaccine that your vet will use will contain a modified dose of the disease that will stimulate your dog's immune system to produce antibodies that will be able to fight the disease. If your puppy is unwell, it may be a good idea to postpone his injections for a while, to minimise the small risk of an adverse reaction. Most vaccines are injected into the scruff, but the kennel cough vaccine is given as drops into the nose. The kennel cough vaccine is usually only given to dogs that will be left in boarding kennels, but it may also be useful if your dog needs to go into hospital for any reason.

When you take your unvaccinated puppy to the vet, you should make sure that you carry him and do not put him down in the surgery. If you plan to put your dog into a boarding kennel, you will need to keep an up-to-date card showing the vaccinations he has had.

ABOVE: *Make sure that you carry your unvaccinated puppy to the vet.*

PUPPY NUTRITION

One of the other most important things you can do for your Stafford puppy is to feed him well. If you have bought your dog from a responsible breeder, they should have given you a diet sheet to follow. If you don't know what your puppy has been eating, you need to buy him some suitable puppy food. These foods are now sometimes breed-specific. It is important that your puppy has access to water at all times but even more so if you are feeding dry food, as these foods can make your dog very thirsty. A common mistake is to give cows' milk to a puppy. This can badly upset your puppy's stomach and give him diarrhoea. Goat's milk is much more palatable to dogs, as it is lower in lactose (to which many are intolerant) and higher in protein. This means that it is much closer to bitch's milk. Fully-weaned puppies don't need milk of any kind.

As your puppy only has a small tummy, you will need to divide your puppy's food into several small meals. Four meals are usually considered best for puppies up to the age of twelve weeks old; breakfast, lunch, tea, and supper. Serving small meals at 7 a.m., 11 a.m., 3 p.m., and 6 or 7 p.m. works quite well. Don't allow your puppy Staffy to go without food for more than six hours in the day. Leave his food down for around ten minutes so that he learns to eat up reasonably quickly. Don't worry if he doesn't finish his food at this age, he may just be

ABOVE: *Follow the diet sheet your breeder gives you when you first get your puppy.*

full. Dried food will swell in the puppy's tummy and he will soon feel satisfied. Leaving his food down for him to graze on is not very salubrious. At this age, intervals of three to four hours between his meals should be about right. Once your puppy is three months old, he can move to three meals a day. By the time he is six months old, two daily meals will be sufficient. When your dog reaches his first birthday, you can move to a single daily meal if you like, but many people prefer to divide their dog's food into two meals a day. If you are unhappy feeding a complete dry diet, you can always supplement this with some tasty treats. Many Stafford owners continue to give their dogs a small breakfast and light supper (as well as the main meal) all their lives, but you need to keep a constant eye on your dog's weight.

Most Staffords have great appetites, and crave tidbits. It is unusual for Staffordshire Bull Terriers to be fussy and you shouldn't struggle to get your puppy eating heartily. Although modern complete diets are extremely convenient, and contain everything your puppy needs, some owners prefer a more traditional puppy diet of various nutritious foods. You should not rely on a diet of household scraps as it is very unlikely that this will provide enough nutrition for your puppy to grow up strong and healthy.

If you decide to feed a traditional meat and biscuit diet rather than a complete food, you should be sure to give your dog a vitamin and mineral supplement each day.

If your Stafford puts on a little weight as he ages, you will need to diet him. Being overweight puts unnecessary strain on their heart and joints. Swapping some of his food for cooked green vegetables or changing to a lower calorie version of his usual food should help. You should never give your dog human treats as these can also damage his teeth. Chocolate and sugar should not to be given to any dog. Stick to dog treats and dog biscuits.

ABOVE: *Your Stafford will enjoy playing with sturdy toys.*

PUPPY EXERCISE

Your new Staffordshire Bull Terrier puppy needs to be kept both mentally and physically active to ensure he is stimulated and happy. Bored and under-exercised Staffies will often be naughty and destructive. But he should not be taken out in public until at least two weeks after his final vaccination. Playing in the garden will be fine at this stage. But it is very important to exercise your puppy moderately as his bones are still soft and growing. Over-exercising a puppy can lead to damage and he will also tire quickly.

As your Stafford matures, exercise will become an increasingly important part of his day. Although he will appreciate long walks, he will also appreciate variety. You can also take toys with you on his walk, so that you can play with these as you go. A Stafford needs at least an hour's exercise every day, and would almost certainly prefer to have more than this.

PUPPY TOYS

Because Staffies like to chew it is important to make sure that anything you give your puppy has been tested for its resilience. Pull toys might spoil his teeth, so these may be best avoided. Squeaky toys should have the squeaker removed in case this gets swallowed. Small balls are also dangerous. Large balls and chew toys made out of tough rubber are best

ABOVE: *Playing in the garden will be fine at this stage but it is very important to exercise your puppy moderation as his bones are still soft and growing.*

and homemade toys such as cardboard boxes will give your puppy hours of harmless fun.

WORMING

Worming is another important aspect of caring for your puppy Stafford. All dogs have worms at some point in their lives, and puppies are at the most risk from infestation. Worms are passed from the mother even before birth and through their milk. They then live in the puppy's intestine and feed on partly digested food. Untreated worms can cause serious illnesses in puppies, including weight loss, vomiting, diarrhoea, swollen tummies and even death. An infested puppy cannot get the benefit from his food and will not thrive. He may also cough and his coat may look dull. Puppies need regular worming to combat this and should be wormed from two weeks of age at two weekly intervals until they are twelve weeks of age, then every month until they are six months of age. Worming should continue at least three times a year with a recommended veterinary preparation for the rest of the dog's life.

Dogs are prone to two main types of worms, tapeworms and roundworms. Roundworms can appear like elastic bands, and grow up to several inches in length. Tapeworms can appear like white grains of rice, which are joined together to form a tape. These are most commonly found in adult dogs and very rarely in puppies.

Your breeder should tell you about the worming programme they have been using and when the next treatment is due. It may be a good plan to let your puppy settle down before you worm him again. Twelve weeks is usually considered to be a good age for this. Your vet can recommend a good product to use. Roundworms are spread through the environment while tapeworms are commonly

spread by fleas, so it is wise to treat an infested dog with a flea treatment. Climate change has meant that dogs are now subject to new types of worm, Angiostrongylus (lungworms), for example. These worms can live in the lungs or in the major blood vessels and may even cause death. Ordinary worming medicine does not work against these parasites. You should check with your vet to see which worms are problematic locally. He may need to prescribe a special treatment to get rid of these.

ABOVE: *Keep your puppy worm-free with advice from your vet.*

4 GROOMING YOUR STAFFORDSHIRE BULL TERRIER

One of the first things to do with your new Staffy puppy is to get him used to being handled, so that you can do essential things such as clean his teeth and cut his nails.

TEETH CLEANING

A Stafford will usually get his adult teeth at around the age of four-and-a-half months. You need to check which puppy teeth are loose and which have fallen out, and to see how the new ones are coming on. Gently lift the lips to check the teeth. Be especially careful if your puppy is teething. It

is good to get your puppy used to this procedure so that both you and your vet will be able to examine his mouth without too much trouble. You should check the tongue to make sure that it looks normal, and check the dog's teeth and gums. The teeth should be clean and free from tartar. If tartar builds up on the teeth his breath will smell, the teeth will become discoloured and eventually the gums will be affected, leading to infection.

You can clean your dog's teeth with a special canine toothbrush, or a small piece of gauze wrapped around your

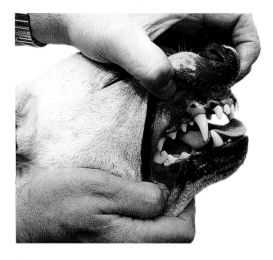

LEFT: *Handle your puppy gently and often so that he gets used to checks like this.*

RIGHT: *Regular checks should ensure your Stafford keeps happy and healthy.*

ABOVE: *A special toothpaste and a soft brush are best for your dog's teeth.*

him with treats and praise when he is cooperative, he will come to accept this as part of his usual routine.

EYE CARE

Your Staffy's eyes should always be bright and clear and free from any foreign objects. You need to check your dog's eyes regularly as eye problems can be indicative of other health problems. You should watch out for excessive crustiness, tearing, red or white eyelid linings, tear-stained hair, closed eyes, cloudiness, a visible third eyelid, or unequal pupil size. If you see of these eye symptoms, you should contact your vet immediately.

finger. A soft brush will avoid scratching the dog's gums. You can get special dog toothpaste from your vet (or on-line). This comes in various tasty flavours, such as chicken. Alternatively, you can use a paste of baking soda and water. Don't use fluoride toothpaste on puppies under the age of six months, as this can interfere with the formation of his dental enamel. Human toothpaste should also be avoided as this can upset your dog's stomach.

Teeth cleaning chews and rawhide toys can help keep the tartar build up down.

Remember, there is no point wrestling with your dog to get his teeth clean. If you can start cleaning his teeth at an early age, and reward

ABOVE: *Your dog's eyes should be clear with no crusting or weeping.*

CLIPPING NAILS

Unless your Staffy spends a lot of time walking on hard surfaces that will help to keep his claws short, his nails will need regular clipping. If you hear them clicking on

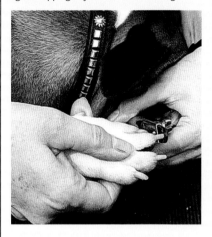

a hard surface, it's time for a trim. Most dogs dislike having their feet handled, so you should try to get your puppy used to this from an early age. A dog's claw is made up of the nail itself, and the quick, which provides the blood supply to the nail. Avoid cutting into the quick as it will bleed profusely and is very sensitive. Don't worry if you can't do all your dog's nails in one session, it might be best to clip one paw at a time, with other activities in between.

You should only use clippers designed for cutting dogs' claws, as human nail clippers will be too small and weak. You may also want to have some styptic powder on hand to coagulate any blood from any minor cuts. Flour can be used in an emergency.

CARING FOR YOUR STAFFY'S COAT

Staffies have short and smooth hair, although some dogs have denser coats than others. A quick brush over every couple of days should be sufficient for this breed. Staffords do shed, so regular grooming is important to keep his coat clean and free of dead hair. This will also stop too much hair being strewn around your home. Grooming can also be a great bonding experience between you and your dog.

If your dog needs to be bathed, you should ensure that you use only dog shampoo as human shampoo is usually too harsh to be used on your dog's coat. You can also buy special

ABOVE: *Check for any bumps or scratches as you groom your dog.*

dog conditioner to lock moisture into the dog's coat and skin. This will prevent all of the natural oils being stripped from his coat.

When brushing your dog, it is usually easier to work backwards from the nose to the tail. Check for any lumps, bumps, or discharges as you go. You can use a soft rubber or plastic curry brush to groom your dog, or a soft bristle brush. This will loosen dust and dead hair from the dog's coat. A close-toothed metal rake can also be used to take out dead hair from close to the skin. This tool should be used with great care to make sure that it

doesn't scratch your dog's skin. You should also take this opportunity to clean your dog's ears with cotton wool and either a special veterinary ear cleaning product, or olive oil. Wipe away any dirt from the flap of the ear. Never insert cotton buds or any other foreign object into your dog's ear. This can be very dangerous and painful.

UNWANTED VISITORS
Unfortunately, even clean and well-groomed dogs can fall victim to several parasites including fleas, lice, ticks, ear mites and harvest mites.

FLEAS

Fleas are small, flat, wingless, blood-sucking insects that are an irritation to dogs and their owners alike. They can also can carry and transmit serious diseases and other parasites (such as tapeworms). They are also the leading cause of skin problems in domestic dogs. Although they can't fly, fleas have powerful rear legs and can jump to extraordinary lengths. There are many types of flea, all of which reproduce rapidly and profusely. Despite its name, the ordinary cat flea is by far the most common flea that bothers pet dogs. Dogs become infested if good flea prevention isn't followed. Dogs can also get fleas by having contact with other animals that have a flea problem. Fortunately, there are many things that dog owners can do to keep fleas under control. Most dogs that have fleas will find them irritating and will scratch, but some can have a severe reaction to flea bites (flea dermatitis). If you think that you have found flea debris in your dog's coat, collect some of the black grit from the coat and put it on a white tissue. If the black grit goes blood-coloured when you dampen it, your

dog has fleas. Wash the dog as quickly as possible, not forgetting his bedding and around the house. There are many excellent flea-control preparations on the market today, but your vet will probably be able to sell you the most effective.

TICKS

Ticks can sometimes be found in your dog's coat in the summer months. Ticks are parasites of sheep and cattle. The adult tick starts life small and spider-like. It crawls over the body, finds a suitable place and bites into the skin. It will stay in this position for about two weeks until fully engorged with blood, swollen to the size of a pea and beige in colour. The tick will then drop off the host and, if female,

ABOVE: *Check for ticks when your dog has been through long grass.*

lay eggs in the grass. These hatch into larvae which will then find a host. After a feed, these larvae drop off, undergo change and find another host. It takes three larvae changes, each taking a year, before the adult form is arrived at and the cycle is then repeated. Ticks can be removed by using flea-control remedies, some of which are also designed to remove ticks. Other methods involve removing the tick with special forceps, making sure you grasp the head. This is made easier by killing the tick first. If you don't manage to remove the tick's mouth parts, the bite can become infected.

LICE
Lice are grey, about 2mm long and they lay small eggs (nits) which stick to the dog's hair and can look like scurf. Dogs can then scratch and create bald patches. You should give your dog repeat treatments of insecticide sprays or baths to kill the adults and any hatching larvae.

HARVEST MITES
Harvest mites infestation occurs in the late summer, starting around late July. They are little orange mites which affect the feet, legs and skin of the tummy and can cause immense irritation. The orange mite can just be seen with a naked eye. Treat with benzyl benzoate, a white emulsion which can be bought at the chemist, which should be rubbed

into the affected parts. Many of the flea insecticides will also treat this complaint.

EAR MITES
Waxy deposits in the ears may mean that your dog has ear mites, especially if he is scratching. Ear drops can get rid of them and regular application should keep them away.

MANGE
Mange is a skin condition that can create severe pain and itching. It can lead to scaling and scabbing and can become infected and pussy. It is caused by a mite that burrows into the skin and then moves around under the surface of the skin. It can lead to hair loss and thickened, reddened skin. Scaling may appear around the mouth, eyes and front legs if the condition remains untreated. Mange is caused by two different types of mite, sarcoptic mites and demodectic mites. Each type of mange mite requires different medications. The dog will also need to be washed with special shampoos to kill of any remaining mites.

NASAL MITES
Nasal mites, or pneumonyssoides canium, are small mites that can infest dog's noses. They may cause a nasal discharge, sneezing, head shaking, coughing and restlessness. They can only be diagnosed by a vet under a microscope.

ABOVE: *Watch for indications like scratching which may indicate a pest.*

LUNGWORM

Lungworm infection is a growing problem for dogs and their owners. It can cause serious health problems and can even be fatal if it is untreated. Infected dogs can pass on the infection through their faeces. Slugs, snails and foxes have all been implicated in spreading the infection. Numbers of all three of these creatures are rising. Owners are warned to try to stop their dogs accidentally ingesting slugs and snails when they are playing outside, drinking from puddles, eating grass or chewing toys that have been left outside overnight. The symptoms of lungworm infection are extensive. They include coughing, tiredness, poor blood clotting, weight loss, poor appetite, vomiting, diarrhoea, depression, lethargy and seizures. The good news is that once diagnosed, treatment for lungworm infection is simple and effective. Separate preventative products are also available to combat lungworm, as most worming preparations are ineffective against lungworm.

45

5 TRAINING YOUR STAFFORDSHIRE BULL TERRIER

ABOVE: *Make sure you have your puppy's full attention when you want to teach him something.*

Basic obedience is important for any dog, but particularly important to strong and resourceful dogs like Staffordshire Bull Terriers. Although they are headstrong, Staffords are born with a desire to please their humans and tend to take on the character of their families, who they will almost inevitably view as their special pack. The first few weeks after you bring your puppy home are important in setting the tone of your future relationship. It will be completely unnecessary to smack your dog, or punish him in any way. A sharp tone of voice and a firm "No!" should be sufficient. For the highly sociable Staffy, the worst punishment is being ignored by you. You should remember that he is young and although he will certainly make mistakes, he will never be naughty on purpose. When he blunders, you need to forgive and correct him gently. As your puppy grows, it is a good idea to enrol him in local obedience classes, but you can start his training the moment you bring him home to live with you.

HOUSE TRAINING

House training is the first sort of training that you should begin with your puppy. It should start as soon as you first arrive home with him. With vigilance and positive training methods, most puppies quickly learn how to be clean in the house. Being a highly intelligent breed, Staffords are particularly quick to learn.

House training will be easier if your puppy has a settled routine, sleeping and eating at the same times during the day. Puppies usually need to relieve themselves when they wake up, during play, and after meals. You should also watch for signs indicating that your puppy wants to go to the toilet; restlessness, whining, tail raising, sniffing and circling around. You should take your puppy to the same place in the garden on each of these occasions. You should encourage him with a consistent phrase such as "toilet." As soon as the puppy performs you should praise him and play with him. You may be surprised how often your puppy needs to relieve himself, but remember he has only a small bladder at this age. This means that he will find it very difficult to stay clean all night long, so it may be a good idea to leave some newspaper or purpose made absorbent pads (available from your local pet shop) down at night.

If your puppy makes a mistake you need to clean up as well as you can so that no smell lingers. Any lingering odour might give the puppy the idea that he can use that spot for his "business" in the future. While some puppies are easier to house train than others, you should remember that your puppy will not have full bladder control until he is about four months old and should never be punished for making mistakes.

ABOVE: *For the highly sociable Staffy, the worst punishment is being ignored by you.*

NAME TRAINING

The very first thing is to teach your puppy his name. You need to call him over to you with a treat in your hand, or be ready to play. You should sound excited and praise him lavishly when he comes to you. A small tidbit works well for Staffies! If you try to establish "coming when called" at an early age this will become second nature to him, and may save his life in a dangerous situation.

TRAINING TIPS

Before you move on to the next steps of training your puppy to sit, stay and walk to heel etc. there are some basic training tips that are well worth

remembering.

From your first days with your Staffy puppy, you should make sure that he sees you as the dominant animal in the pack. You should be able to touch him whenever you wish, lift him off a bed or chair, take a toy or any other object away from him and touch his food and bowls at all times, even when he is eating. Any growling or adverse reaction should be rebuked immediately.

Once you start your pup's training, you should always make sure that you have his full attention before you give a command. You should aim only to give commands that your puppy will obey, so you need to make sure that he is listening to you. You can do this by calling his name or snapping your fingers until you have good eye contact with him. Then give your command and make sure that your puppy follows through. Give him time to respond but ensure that he does as you have asked. Don't keep repeating the command as this means that your pup chooses when he obeys you. The idea is that he should obey you at once.

Puppies have only a short attention span, so you should keep your training sessions to no more than five or ten minutes. Your puppy won't be able to focus for much longer than this. It's important to keep the atmosphere of the training sessions as positive as possible, with lots of praise. If your puppy seems confused by a new command go back to something you know he can do so that you can end the session on a positive note. If you are using training treats as part of your method you may well find that it's better to time your sessions before meals, when the puppy might be a little hungry. But as your puppy gradually learns your commands you should phase out the treats, as you don't want to have to rely on treats in the long term.

ABOVE: *Give a treat when the puppy responds to a command.*

In training your dog you should try to step into the role of being a positive pack leader or parent to your dog. Bonding with your dog in his early life and encouraging him to mix with other people and animals will help him to be calm and confident when he grows up. Because he will not be protected by his vaccinations in these early weeks you will need to carry him if he goes outside your house and garden. Your attitude is very crucial at this stage in his life. If he has your calm and unqualified support, it will help him to develop into the kind of well socialised dog that will be easy to train.

LEFT: *Your aim is a calm and confident dog.*

Teaching Recall

It is very important (for his own safety) that your puppy will come to you when you call. If you are struggling to get your puppy to come to you, try carrying a treat in a crinkly paper bag. If your puppy doesn't come when you call him you can rustle the bag while you repeat his name. As soon as he has made the connection between the rustling paper and the treat he will always come to you. When he does you should stroke and praise him.

If he doesn't seem to get it, put him on an extending lead while you teach him this exercise. Let the pup run to the length of the lead and then call him back to you. Reward him with a treat

ABOVE: *When he has obeyed you give him a treat and praise him.*

ABOVE: *It is very important that your puppy will come to you when you call.*

and a cuddle.

If your Stafford decides to disobey you use a low firm voice to get his attention. You don't need to shout! Once you have his attention you should immediately change your tone to a soft and encouraging tone and call him again. This should do the trick. When he has obeyed you give him a treat and praise him. You should also remember that however angry your dog has made you by refusing to come when he has been called, you must never punish him when he does finally come to you. This will confuse him and undermine his trust in your leadership.

Lead training

Most Staffords learn how to walk on the lead quite quickly. Their natural inclination is to keep close to you so attaching a lead to your pup's collar is usually no problem. Twelve to fourteen weeks is a good age for a puppy to start wearing his first collar. The puppy's neck will be delicate so you should use a very soft and comfortable collar. Your puppy will soon grow out of this, so wait until he is at least six months of age before you buy him anything expensive.

The best place to begin training your puppy is in your garden. In this safe and controlled environment your puppy can learn about walking on the lead where there is nothing to upset or distract him. Encourage him and praise him as he walks well, but do not allow him to rush forwards and pull. This is very important as a grown Stafford will be a very strong dog. You should aim to be able to walk him with a slack lead. Choke chains are too dangerous for Staffies, and harnesses lose some of the close contact between you and the dog. Try to get him to walk calmly by your side for a few yards, without pulling on the lead. Once he has done this, praise him lavishly. Getting him to walk well on the lead may take some patience and determination, but calm lead work will build a strong bond of

ABOVE: *At twelve weeks your puppy can wear a soft collar and lead training can begin soon after.*

soft puppy collars

trust between you. This means that when he goes out into the world and meets new and scary things he will look to you for reassurance. You have several weeks to work on this exercise before his vaccinations are complete and your Staffy can go into the outside world.

Training to heel

The art of training your Stafford to "heel" is a simple extension of training your puppy to work on the lead. The greater control the exercise gives you over your puppy is particularly important in an urban environment. The object of the exercise is to have the puppy walking by your side with his head level with your left leg.

Start the exercise with your dog close to your left leg, with both of you facing the same way. Have one of your

pup's favourite treats in your left hand. Hold the treat up near your waist, not directly in front of your dog's nose. Now say your dog's name to get his attention and to gain eye contact. Immediately take two steps forward and then stop. If your dog moves with you and is still in the heel position enthusiastically praise him and give a treat.

As soon as your puppy swallows his reward repeat the heeling process again. Say his name and take two steps forward while saying "come on" or "that's a good boy." Then stop, praise your dog and give him a treat. Only ever give the reward when your dog is still in the heel position. It's important to remember that you are using the treat to reward good behaviour rather than to lure or bribe him.

If at any time your dog lags behind or forges ahead of you, hold off with your praise and rewards. Simply start the exercise again.

LEFT: *Teach your Stafford to heel on your left side, level with your leg.*

Teaching the sit

Teaching your puppy to sit is a useful exercise, as it shows him that you are in control. It can also calm a difficult situation. If, however, your puppy does not understand repeat the command "sit" and gently push the puppy's hindquarters down into the sitting position and then reward with a treat. The puppy will learn quickly.

TEACHING THE DOWN
The Down is the next command after Sit. Start with your puppy at the Sit position. Have a treat in your hand which you then hold on the floor in front of the puppy. When the puppy goes down for it give the command "Down" followed by the reward and praise. When this exercise is repeated several times the puppy will go down without you having to put your hand

ABOVE: *Teach your puppy to sit using praise and a treat.*

LEFT: *When your dog is happy to sit on command, you can teach the "Down".*

to the floor, but reward and praise every time until it is firmly established. If the puppy will not go down at the start of this training you can give very gentle pressure on the forequarters to encourage him to go down to the floor.

ABOVE: *The down command.*

53

ABOVE: *A play session is a good reward after training sessions.*

Teaching the stay

Learning to "Stay" is important to all dogs. When you first start to teach your puppy to stay it is best to have him on the lead. Ask the puppy to either sit, or go down, with the lead extended from you to the puppy; walk away backwards (facing the puppy) and repeat the command "Stay". When you get as far as the end of the lead, stand still for a few seconds, ask the puppy

ABOVE: *Use a hand signal to reinforce the "Stay" command. Start training with the lead on and, as the dog learns, remove the lead.*

ABOVE: *Eventually you will be able to command your dog to stay and walk away before recalling him.*

to come, and praise him. Gradually lengthen the distance you leave the puppy and always give praise when he does it right. If the puppy breaks the Stay take him back to where you left him at Sit or Down and repeat the exercise, but do not go so far away from him before you call him. This exercise will take time and patience; little and often is best.

55

6 STAFFORDSHIRE BULL TERRIER SPORTS

The energetic and powerful Staffordshire Bull Terrier has become a popular competitor at many canine competitions, including agility, Flyball and obedience.

COMPETITIVE OBEDIENCE

Many Staffies take part in competitive obedience trials at dog shows around the world. This rewarding sport is the logical extension of good training. Each level of obedience trial has a set list of exercises and requirements for dogs and their handlers to follow as closely as possible. Marks are awarded for the ability of the combined dog/handler team. As well as taking your dog's training to a higher level, competitive obedience can be highly enjoyable for both dogs and humans and a great bonding experience.

AGILITY

Despite some people's preconceptions, Staffords can excel at agility competitions. Their athletic physiques and big personalities shine in the ring! Agility is great exercise for Staffies

BELOW: *Hopping over a hurdle!*

ABOVE: *The dog and handler run round the course together.*

and owners of all ages and keeps the dogs calm by giving them something to concentrate on. It is also a great bonding experience, as Staffies love to work with their handlers and obey their instructions.

Competitive agility dates back to the Crufts dog shows of the late 1970s. To entertain the audience in the interval dogs ran around a specially designed course against the clock. The inspiration behind the concept was competitive horse jumping. The sport quickly spread to the United States and has now spread around the world. The sport consists of a dog and handler running around an obstacle course together. The obstacles are usually all different, but may include a variety of hurdles, an A-frame, a dog-walk, a see-saw, a tunnel, a long jump and a tyre. The competing dog/handler teams are

LEFT:
Scrambling over an A-frame!

57

ABOVE: *These powerful dogs come into their own in flyball competions.*

RIGHT: *The sport is an entertaining way to interact with your Stafford in a fun environment.*

scored for speed and accuracy. The dogs participate off the lead and it is not permissible to encourage them with food or toys. The handler can only use voice and hand signals to instruct their dog.

FLYBALL

Flyball is another competitive canine sport in which Staffordshire Bull Terriers excel. Teams of dogs race against each other over a line of hurdles. The dogs then release and catch a tennis ball when the dog presses a spring-loaded pad. The sport is an entertaining and active way to interact with your Stafford in a fun environment. It is also an effective way to burn off a Staffordshire Bull Terrier's high levels of energy. Flyball has become increasingly popular in recent years and interest in the sport ensures that breeders continue to produce truly athletic Staffies that are strong, quick and agile with a good level of stamina. In Britain the sport is governed by the British Flyball Association and in America the sport is regulated by the North American Flyball Association.

Staffordshire Bull Terriers as Therapy Dogs

Staffies love people so much that they can make great Pets As Therapy (PAT) dogs after the appropriate training. Therapy dogs are usually trained from puppies to be "bombproof" by being exposed to lots of different situations, people and noises. Therapy dogs work with all kinds of different people, including the elderly, disabled and sick. Their loving and kind natures are ideal for this kind of important work and contact with these dogs can be very healing and beneficial.

7 SHOWING YOUR STAFFORDSHIRE BULL TERRIER

If you bought your Stafford puppy from a line of show dogs, you may wish to show him. This will mean that your dog will be compared to your national Staffordshire Bull Terrier breed standard. This lays down the ideal character, temperament and appearance for the breed by which your dog will be judged.

The first thing that any good judge will be looking for is a sound and healthy dog that is a good example of the breed. No reputable breeder would allow an unhealthy dog, or a dog with health issues to produce a litter.

Showing your dog can be a great way to make new friends and can be a highly absorbing hobby. Showing

ABOVE: *If your Stafford came from a line of show dogs, you may wish to show him.*

ABOVE: *Showing your dog can be an absorbing hobby.*

Staffordshire Bull Terriers has become very popular in recent years and local breed organisations hold many shows around the country. These include all kinds of dog shows from the informal to the highly competitive and there are also parallel events for young dog handlers. So long as you approach dog shows with good sportsmanship and a sense of humour they can be great fun. You will need a small amount of equipment to show your dog. This should include a good grooming kit, a show lead, and a water bowl. You may find it safe and convenient to take your dog to shows in a dog crate. At the show itself the judge will want to check your dog over and see him in action

63

ABOVE: *It is a good idea to attend a dog show before you enter one just to see what happens.*

moving around the show ring. In Britain all dog shows are regulated by the Kennel Club.

Before you show your own dog it is a very good idea to attend a dog show and see what will be expected of you and your Stafford. This will also give you a good idea of how Staffordshire

ABOVE: *Arrive in good time so that your dog can settle down*

ABOVE: *The judge will inspect your dog starting at the dog's head.*

Bull Terriers are prepared for showing.

Most dog shows ask their participants to fill in a set of entry forms. You need to fill in these show entry forms very carefully, as mistakes may mean disqualification. In the UK your dog also needs to be Kennel Club-registered in your name before you can show him. Novice owners may think that if a dog has been registered by the breeder he can be shown. But this is not the case. Make sure that you arrive at the show in good time so that you and your dog can settle down in the busy atmosphere and relax. Your dog will need to be at least six months of age before he can be entered into a show.

Dog show judges all have their own system of judging, but most will ask participants to line up as a class. The judge will then ask you all to move together before inspecting the dogs individually. They will then ask you to move your dog on his own so that he can give him a full inspection. Most judges start their examination at the dog's head. This will include looking at your Stafford's mouth to see if he has the breed's correct bite. The judge will feel the body, forequarters and hindquarters. He will also check your dog's paws, pads and his tail. The judge, with both hands, will span the dog behind the shoulders and assess his weight.

The judge will then ask you to move the dog around the ring. He might

ABOVE: *You will need to stand your dog squarely on his feet or "stack" him, for his inspection by the judge.*

ask you to move up and down, or in a triangle. This is so that he can assess the dog's movement from the front and rear and in profile. When the judge has reached a decision, he will place the dogs in order of merit. Don't take it too badly if you don't win on this occasion, you and your Stafford may be more lucky next time you venture into the show ring.

There are several things you should do to train your Stafford for the show

ring. Attending local ring craft classes is one way to do this, but you can do a lot of his training yourself.

One of the things you will need to know how to do is to "stack" your dog. "Stacking" puts the dog into a position where he can be examined by a show judge. Your dog needs to able to stand "four square" so that if a judge stands above him, he won't be able to see legs or paws sticking out.

ABOVE: *The judge will watch the dog's gait from all sides.*

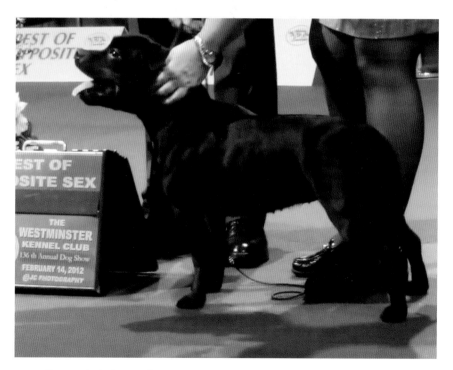

ABOVE: *You may be lucky enough to win a prize.*

The Breed Standard

RIGHT: *Smooth coated, well balanced and of great strength for its size.*

Your dog must also conform as closely as possible to the Kennel Club breed standard for Staffordshire Bull Terriers. His general appearance should show him to be well-balanced, muscular, active and agile with great strength for his size. He should also demonstrate the typical personality characteristics of the breed: courage, tenacity, boldness, fearlessness and intelligence. He should also have an affectionate nature, especially with children.

Physically, your Stafford should be of one of the approved breed colours: red, fawn, white, black, blue or any one of these colours combined with white.

His coat should be healthy, dense and smooth. It should cling closely to his body to give your dog a streamlined appearance. Size wise, he should be between 36 and 41 centimetres high at the withers. Dogs should weigh between 13 and 17 kilograms and bitches should weigh between 11 and 15.4 kilograms.

To conform to the breed stand for Staffordshire Bull Terriers, your dog's head should be short, deep and broad with pronounced cheek muscles and a distinct stop. He should also have a short muzzle and a black nose. His eyes should be dark with dark rims, round, medium-sized, and his gaze should be fixed straight ahead. Your Stafford should have rose or half-pricked ears. Ears that are full, drooping or pricked are incorrect for the breed. His lips should be tight and clean and his jaws strong. Staffordshire Bull Terriers should have large teeth with a perfect and regular scissor bite. His neck should be short and muscular, widening towards the shoulders. His legs should be straight and well-boned, set wide apart, with slightly out-turned feet. The shoulders should be laid back. His hindquarters should be well muscled, and his back legs should be parallel when viewed from behind. His feet should be medium-

sized, strong and well padded with black nails. A Stafford's body should be close-coupled with a level top line and wide front. His ribs should be well spring, muscular and well defined. His tail should be of a medium length and taper to a point. It should be low-set and carried low. It should also be fairly straight, without too much curl. Male dogs should have two testicles fully descended in the scrotum.

In the show ring, a Stafford's bearing should be free, powerful and agile and his legs should move in parallel. Staffies have a reputation for being very active dogs and show dogs need to look fit and toned.

RIGHT: *The breed requires the head to be short with a broad skull, very pronounced cheek muscles and short foreface.*

8 STAFFORDSHIRE BULL TERRIER HEALTH ISSUES

Although a healthy Staffordshire Bull Terrier can live for between ten and sixteen years, the breed is prone to several health issues. It is possible to screen for several of these, and responsible breeders will do this.

THE INBREEDING COEFFICIENT – COI

COI stands for the Coefficient of Inbreeding. Essentially, this is a measure of how much inbreeding occurs within a particular breed. The lower this is, the better, as it means that the chances of puppies inheriting genetic illnesses from closely-related parents is lower. For Staffords, the COI is 6.7%. Unfortunately, irresponsible breeding has enabled several genetic illnesses to become prevalent among Staffies.

Hip Dysplasia The mean score for hip dysplasia in Staffordshire Bull Terriers is 12.9, which is a relatively low (good) score. You should ask for the score of your puppy's parents and make sure that it is comparable to this. If their scores are much higher than this, you may wish to re-consider buying this particular puppy.

Brachycephalic Upper Airway Syndrome This is a serious condition that arises from facial/skull abnormalities. It affects the dog's ability to breathe and can make it difficult for affected animals to take the exercise they need. The worse the abnormality, the harder breathing will be. Mildly affected dogs will have noisy breathing and may snort when they are excited and snore when they are asleep. Badly affected dogs will tire very easily during exercise and may even faint or collapse. They may also cough, gag, retch and even vomit. Ultimately, the condition can also put a

fatal strain on the dog's heart.

Dogs and bitches can both be affected by this condition and affected animals are usually diagnosed at an early age, usually before they reach their fourth birthday. Their symptoms may be aggravated by humid weather.

EYE DISEASES
Unfortunately, Staffords are prone to several serious eye conditions. These include:

1 **Persistent hyperplastic primary vitreous (PHPV) cataracts.** This condition can cause serious lesions on the eye that can result in sight loss. Both of your puppy's parents should have been screened for the condition and the breeder should be able to show you a certificate for this.
2 **Hereditary cataracts (HC1-HSF4).** A DNA test is also available for this condition. Hereditary cataracts can affect dogs from an early age. They are usually treated by surgery. The prognosis for cataract surgery is better if this is done at an early stage in the development of the cataract. Dogs that have undergone surgery are usually hospitalised for a couple of days before they are sent home. Dogs that have been diagnosed with cataracts should not be bred from.

Organic Aciduria Organic Aciduria (L-2-HGA) is a serious condition that affects the central nervous system. It is

a metabolic disorder that disrupts the amino acid metabolism and causes a build of acid in the tissues. Its effects may manifest at an early age. The disease can cause a range of distressing symptoms, including epileptic seizures, wobbliness, and changed behaviour. A DNA test is available for this condition.

Demodicosis Staffords are also prone to demodicosis. This horrible condition is also known as demodectic mange or red mange. It is a skin problem caused by the demodex mite. The mite occurs in the hair follicles of most dogs and can reproduce rapidly if the dog's immune system is compromised. The results of this illness can range from minor skin irritation and hair loss to a severe and widespread inflammation that can even be life-threatening. Severe demodicosis is usually treated by drugs.

Mast Cell Tumour Staffords are sadly prone to mast cell tumours. This is a cancer of the immune system that can be either malignant or benign. The disease can result in localised tumours in the skin that can be itchy and painful to a severe and painful condition where the cancer affects the dog's internal organs or digestive tract. There is no screening test for the condition. The average age for a Stafford to be diagnosed with this condition is eight, but even puppies can be affected. Early diagnosis is important for effective treatment. Untreated, the condition can be fatal.

Canine Follicular Dysplasia
Canine follicular dysplasia is also known as seasonal flank alopecia. This is a hair loss condition. There is currently no test to screen for this condition. The hair loss is caused by a structural abnormality in the dog's hair follicles. Diagnosis is by biopsy, and there are no effective treatments for the condition. Staffords are particularly prone to the condition, along with the Mexican Hairless Dog and Chinese Crested Dog.

ABOVE: *Responsible breeders screen their breeding stock for diseases.*

Common Canine Ailments and Injuries

Staffordshire Bull Terriers can also be affected by common canine ailments and injuries. These include several conditions that owners should look out for.

Anal glands: A dog's anal glands are located on either side of the anus. Their original use was for scent marking. As a rule these glands are emptied by defecation but, if the dog's motions are soft and too loose, there is not the pressure on the glands which is needed to clear them. An affected dog will drag his rear end along the floor, or will attempt to chew or lick near his tail area in order to relieve the irritation caused by overfilled anal glands. An abscess may occur if they are not cleaned. If you are unable to empty them yourself, it would be advisable to get your vet to do it for the dog's comfort.

Arthritis: This is a complaint that usually affects older dogs. A veteran Stafford may endure stiffness, but do not allow the dog to suffer unnecessarily as there are several remedies that greatly benefit this complaint.

Burns and scalds: The treatment for burns and scalds is the same as for humans. Rinse the affected area under a cold tap or hosepipe in order to take the heat out. In minor cases apply a suitable soothing ointment; in serious cases your vet must be consulted. A badly burned dog will be suffering from shock and should be kept warm and quiet in his bed or box.

Constipation: If this happens frequently it probably indicates incorrect feeding, so you may want to adjust your feeding regime. Gnawing bones can also cause this problem in some dogs. Changing your dog's exercise patterns can sometimes cause constipation. Dogs are creatures of habit and, if they have to wait too long to pass a motion, this can cause constipation. When a dog is constipated, occasionally it will pass a smearing of blood with the motion. As long as it is only a trace it will resolve itself but, if there is any considerable amount then it should be considered serious. Home remedies for an odd incident of constipation include a small amount of olive oil, mineral oil, or milk. You should also make sure that your dog is drinking enough water as this in itself can cause constipation. If the attack lasts for longer than twenty-four hours or the dog seems to be straining excessively, you should consult your vet immediately as this may indicate a blockage.

Diarrhoea: There can be many reasons for this condition. The dog's diet, a change of diet, or eating something nasty can start a bout of diarrhoea. This can usually be stopped by fasting the dog for twenty-four hours. You should give him a solution of glucose and water to drink so that he does not become dehydrated. Start feeding again with light, easy-to-digest foods such as chicken or fish. Diarrhoea can also be a sign of serious problems such as gastroenteritis, parvovirus, worm infestation, foreign bodies in the gut or internal organ problems. Stress can also trigger diarrhoea, just as it can in humans. You should monitor your dog closely while he suffers from diarrhoea, and if a bout turns into something more persistent you should take him to the vet. Unattended diarrhoea can lead to your dog becoming dehydrated and extremely ill.

Fits: There are a considerable number of reasons why dogs fit. Puppies that are infested with worms can fit. Once de-wormed they never fit again. Puppies may also have a reaction to their vaccinations and this can bring on a fit. This is rare but you should report it to your vet. He should be able

to correct the problem. A fitting dog can be a very distressing sight. He may collapse, and may froth at the mouth. He may also go rigid and his legs may start to move as though he was running. He may also lose control over his bladder and bowels. While this is happening do not interfere, but ensure the dog can do no harm to himself while thrashing about. When the dog comes out of a fit he will be extremely weak and confused and will stand and walk as if drunk. Put the dog, at this point, in a safe, enclosed, darkened place where he will be quiet until he has recovered. If the dog has another fit you should definitely take him to

your vet. If epilepsy is diagnosed there are drugs that will control it.

Heatstroke: This is an acute emergency which happens during hot weather. It mostly occurs in dogs that have been shut inside a hot car. A dog should never be put in a hot car in warm weather, even with the windows well open. A car will turn into an oven on a warm day and the temperature inside the car will increase rapidly. A dog can become severely distressed in minutes and die very, very quickly. Even on much cooler days the windows must be left wide open and grills fitted. A heatstroke victim will be severely distressed, frantically panting and will probably collapse. His temperature will be extremely high and, to bring it down, the dog's body should be submerged in cool water or hosed down with water. Do not use very cold water as this will cause more problems. When the temperature returns to normal the dog should be dried and put in a cool place to recover. The dog should have drinking water available at all stages, preferably with salt added (one dessertspoonful of salt per litre of water). If the dog does not recover quickly it would be advisable to take him to the vet as he may be suffering from shock.

Lameness: Dogs will go lame for many reasons but the most common causes are found in the foot. If your dog is lame, check the pads for cuts, cracks, dried mud between the pads, thistles or any kind of swelling. Check the nails have not been damaged or that the nail bed is not infected. Sores between the pads can also cause lameness. If you find a foreign body in the foot, remove it and clean the foot with warm antiseptic water. An infected nail bed will need antibiotic treatment from the vet. This condition is very painful and should be treated quickly. If it isn't treated, the nail can drop off, which can cause further serious problems. A damaged nail, if down to the nail bed, should be bandaged to stop the dog knocking it further. Be extremely careful when you bandage your dog's feet. This can do serious harm if it is done

incorrectly. Get professional help if in doubt.

If nothing appears wrong in the foot you must start to go up the leg, feeling for any swellings, lumps or cuts. Feel the opposite leg and compare the shape and size. Find out if there is any difference in the heat of the legs; bend the joints and move the leg. The dog may or may not flinch when you touch the injury. Some dogs will be lame one day and, after resting overnight, will be completely sound the next. However, if the cause of your dog's lameness is still undetected and has not improved after two days you should take him to your vet.

The Veteran Staffordshire Bull Terrier

A Staffordshire Bull Terrier has an average life expectancy of between ten and fifteen or sixteen. Birth to two years old is usually considered to be the growth stage, two years to five years old the young adult stage, five to eight years middle age, and eight years plus old age. Of course, as any dog gets older he may well need more day-to-day care and veterinary treatment.

To many owners their veteran Stafford will become even more precious as he ages. He will have given the best years of his life to be your companion. There are still some lovely times that you can have together as Staffords can live to a good age.

As your dog ages his needs will change and the way you care for him will need to keep up with this. Good sense will tell you how much exercise he wants. A dog over the age of eight should be taken for shorter walks at his old pace. Of course, each dog will age at his own rate, so discretion and discernment is required.

Diet is perhaps one of the important changes you will notice as your dog ages. He will no longer require as much food. His teeth may not be as good as they were, so an entirely hard diet may no longer be suitable. It might also suit your older dog to eat two smaller meals each day so that his digestive system can cope better. Many dog food manufacturers offer diets that have been specially designed for the older dog. These may well be appropriate for your older Staffordshire Bull Terrier.

If your dog is taking less exercise you may also find that you need to trim his nails more often, and you need to make absolutely sure that you keep his coat clean. Grooming will also give you a chance to check him over and notice any health problems at an early stage.

Older Staffords should always be kept comfortable and warm. You should never allow your older dog to get cold and wet. Make sure his bed is somewhere where the temperature is constant and free of draughts. He will sleep longer and more soundly than when he was younger. If you have younger dogs in the family make sure the old dog is not left out but, at the same time, do not let the young dogs either annoy or disturb the old dog when he is sleeping. You should also protect the old dog from any over-boisterous activities from the younger dogs.

Although every day with your

veteran dog is precious, if your Stafford is failing in health and losing his quality of life you may need to consider putting him to sleep. Your vet will help you make that decision when the time comes. It is the hardest decision to make but don't let your dog suffer at the end; you owe it to him to have a dignified and painless departure from the world.

Summary

Staffies are now highly regarded by many people and have a wonderful reputation for their indomitable courage, intelligence, and affectionate nature with children. The British Kennel Club describes the breed as "Bold, fearless and totally reliable." It is one of only two breeds that are officially recognized by the Kennel Club as being good with children. They have a great reputation as fantastic family pets that adore their families and are wonderful around children. Staffies do need their daily exercise even more than many other dog breeds. They have high energy levels and the more exercise they get the calmer and better behaved they will be.